## Stupendous and Tremendous SCIENCE

# Powerful (and Pungent) Plants

### Enter a world of fantastic flora!

**Claudia Martin**

Please visit our website,
www.garethstevens.com.
For a free color catalog of all
our high-quality books, call
toll free 1-800-542-2595 or
fax 1-877-542-2596.

Cataloging-in-Publication Data

Names: Martin, Claudia.
Title: Powerful (and pungent) plants / Claudia Martin.
Description: Buffalo, NY : Gareth Stevens Publishing, 2025. |
Series: Stupendous and tremendous science |
Includes glossary and index.
Identifiers: ISBN 9781482468816 (pbk.) |
ISBN 9781482468823 (library bound) |
ISBN 9781482468830 (ebook)
Subjects: LCSH: Plants--Juvenile literature. | Plant anatomy--
Juvenile literature. | Pollination--Juvenile literature.
Classification: LCC QK49.M37 2025 | DDC 580--dc23

Published in 2025 by
**Gareth Stevens Publishing**
2544 Clinton St.
Buffalo, NY 14224

First published in Great Britain in 2022 by Wayland

Copyright © Hodder and Stoughton Limited, 2022

**Author and editor:**
Claudia Martin

**Series designer:**
Rocket Design (East Anglia) Ltd

**Illustrator:**
Steve Evans

Illustrations by Steve Evans: front cover main, 2, 5c, 9b, 11tr, 11b, 13cl, 17cl, 17cr, 20cr, 21c, 22t, 25cl, 26b, 28b, 29t, 29c, 29b, 31br.

Picture acknowledgements: iStock: blueringmedia 4; Shutterstock: BudOlga front cover tr, back cover cl, GraphicsRF.com front cover b/g, 1, 7cr, drawkman 3t, 16c, 30tl, Gabi Wolf 3b, Nickolay Stanev 5r, Excellent Dream 6, Basjan Bernard 7tr, Africa Studio 7cl, Budai Romi 7b, Bahdanovich Alena 8, Studio Barcelona 9t, Unicus 9cr, Dobryanska Olga 10tl, Ortis 10tr, Oleg Krugliak 10c, Julia Sudnitskaya 10bl, Muellek Josef 10br, Vecton 12, Christian Vinces 13cr, Sari ONeal 13br, Flower Studio 13bc, MicroOne 14–15c, Vector Tradition 14t, Daniel Prudek 14br, Yayayoyo 15tr, Ondrej Prosicky 15cl, Drosophila Photograph 15c, Nattanan726 15cr, Danita Delimont 15b, taveesak srisomthavil 17c, Tetiana Maltseva 17br, Jason Finn 18cr, Robert Neumann 18cl, K.Pock Pics 18br, ervin herman 18bl, AlexeyZet 19tr, DSLucas 19bl, Henri Koskinen 20bl, lorenza62 20br, Kuttelvaserova Stuchelova 21bl, Kris Wiktor 21br, Aysezgicmeli 22bc, Muh Sahal Mahadi 22br, plasid 23tr, I. Rottlaender 23cl, jflin98 23cr, nnattalli 23bl, KatyGr5 24cr, 32br, Volodymyr Nikolaiev 24br, Tiger Images 24bc, Lubava 24br, Zmiter 25tr, 32t, Gavran333 25bl, Egor Rodynchenko 25bc, Subject Photo 25br, Shanvood 26cl, Jerry Horbert 27tl, Tjis 27tr, Jiang Tianmu 27cl, Ion Mes 27cr.

All additional design elements from Shutterstock or drawn by designer.

Every effort has been made to clear copyright.
Should there be any inadvertent omission, please apply to the publisher for rectification.

The website addresses (URLs) included in this book were valid at the time of going to press. However, it is possible that contents or addresses may have changed since the publication of this book. No responsibility for any such changes can be accepted by either the author or the publisher. All facts and statistics were up to date at the time of press.

All rights reserved. No part of this book may be reproduced in any form without permission in writing from the publisher, except by a reviewer.

Printed in the United States of America

CPSIA compliance information: Batch #CW25GS: For further information contact Gareth Stevens at 1-800-542-2595.

# POWERFUL AND PUNGENT CONTENTS

PLOP

| | |
|---|---|
| Precious Plants | 4 |
| Daring to be Different | 6 |
| Get to the Root of It | 8 |
| Leave It! | 10 |
| Fierce Flowers | 12 |
| Powerful Pollination | 14 |
| Weird Fruit | 16 |
| Strange Seeds | 18 |
| Killer Plants | 20 |
| Don't Eat Me! | 22 |
| Funky Feeders | 24 |
| Oddly Useful | 26 |
| Astonishing Activity: Colorful Leaves | 28 |
| Glossary | 30 |
| Further Reading | 31 |
| Index | 32 |

# PRECIOUS PLANTS

From prickly cacti to bushy ferns, there are around 375,000 species of plants. What do they have in common? Most plants are green and have an amazing superpower: They make their own food.

## HOW DO PLANTS MAKE FOOD?

Plants make food from three ingredients: sunlight, water, and **carbon dioxide**, which is a gas they **absorb** from the air. Sunlight is energy given off by the Sun. Plants soak up sunlight through their **leaves** using a green chemical called **chlorophyll**, which is why most plants look green. Using this energy, plants change carbon dioxide and water into sugar and **oxygen**. This superpower is called **photosynthesis**, which means "making from light" in Greek.

ENERGY

CARBON DIOXIDE

OXYGEN

SUGAR (MADE INSIDE LEAVES)

WATER

### FREAKY FACT

The oldest living thing is believed to be a bristlecone pine that is over 5,000 years old. These trees grow in stony soils in parts of the United States where there is little rain.

# WHAT'S THE POINT OF PLANTS?

By changing sunlight into food, plants create a type of energy that animals can use. Plant-eating animals eat plants to get energy to live … and that energy is passed on to the meat-eaters that eat them! On top of that, when plants photosynthesize, they release oxygen. Humans and other animals need oxygen to survive.

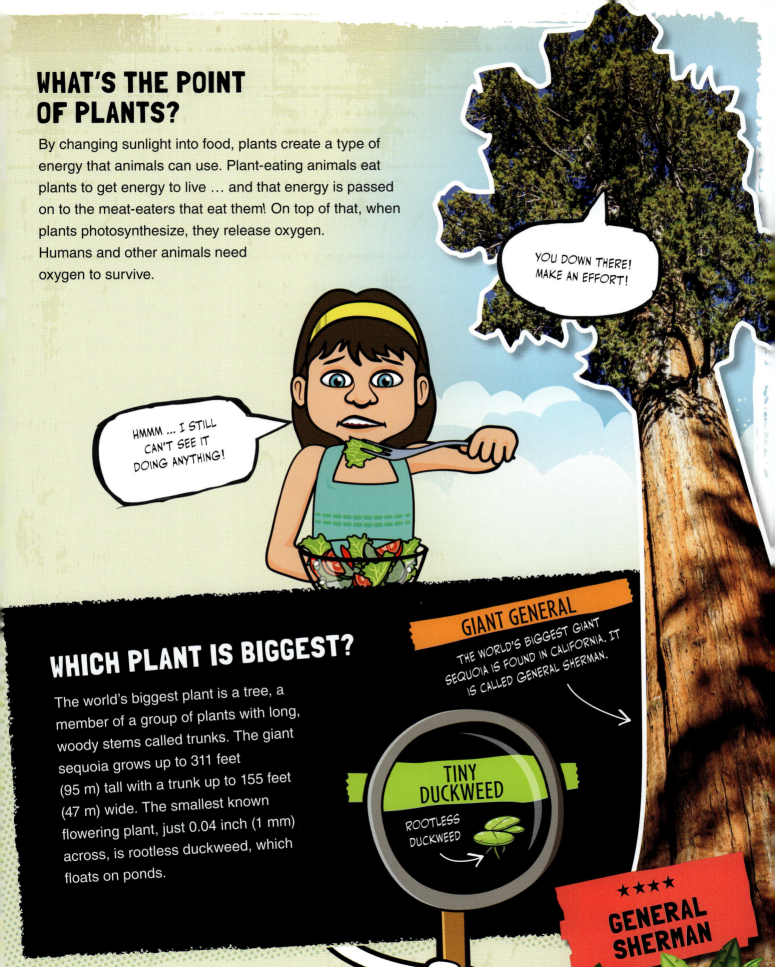

YOU DOWN THERE! MAKE AN EFFORT!

HMMM … I STILL CAN'T SEE IT DOING ANYTHING!

## WHICH PLANT IS BIGGEST?

The world's biggest plant is a tree, a member of a group of plants with long, woody stems called trunks. The giant sequoia grows up to 311 feet (95 m) tall with a trunk up to 155 feet (47 m) wide. The smallest known flowering plant, just 0.04 inch (1 mm) across, is rootless duckweed, which floats on ponds.

### GIANT GENERAL

THE WORLD'S BIGGEST GIANT SEQUOIA IS FOUND IN CALIFORNIA. IT IS CALLED GENERAL SHERMAN.

TINY DUCKWEED

ROOTLESS DUCKWEED

★★★★
GENERAL SHERMAN

# DARING to be DIFFERENT

With a little sunlight, warmth, and water, plants can survive in **habitats** from oceans to deserts. Yet in different habitats, plants have found different ways to survive – which has given us a marvelous mix of plants!

## DO ALL PLANTS HAVE THE SAME PARTS?

Most – but not all – plants have **roots**, **stems**, and leaves. Although they look surprisingly different from each other, roses, trees, grasses, and ferns all have these parts. These are **vascular** plants, which have roots to draw up water from the soil and tiny tubes to transport it around their body.

THERE ARE AROUND 310,000 SPECIES OF VASCULAR PLANTS.

# DO ALL PLANTS FLOWER?

Most vascular plants have **flowers**. Flowers produce **seeds**, which contain the **embryo** of a new plant. Non-flowering plants make seeds without the help of flowers. Many, including conifers, produce seeds in cones. Others, such as ferns, **reproduce** by releasing spores instead of seeds. Spores are tinier and simpler than seeds.

I THOUGHT ALL PLANTS HAD FLOWERS!

CONIFER CONE

MY SEEDS WILL FALL OUT IF YOU SHAKE ME!

SHAKE IT OUT!

FERN

SPORES

# SURELY ALL PLANTS HAVE ROOTS?

In fact, there are around 65,000 species of rootless plants, including mosses. They usually live in damp places or in water, so they can soak up water through hair-like rhizoids. If these plants live on land, their rhizoids also anchor them to the ground. These simple plants reproduce using spores.

MOSS

## SUPER SCIENCE

*Syntrichia caninervis* is a moss that survives in deserts, where it hardly ever rains. Since *Syntrichia* has no roots, it collects tiny drops of water from fog in its cup-like, hairy leaves. This method of water-collection is being borrowed by scientists to build machines that supply drinking water to people in dry regions.

# GET to the ROOT of IT

Roots hold a plant in place and soak up water through their thin, hair-like tips. Whether superlong or stealthy, roots have many ways to get the job done.

## WHICH PLANT HAS THE LONGEST ROOTS?

Roots also allow a plant to soak up **nutrients**, such as nitrogen, which are found in soil. In dry areas, many plants have long roots that grow deep underground. They are able to reach water that lies far beneath the dry surface soil. The longest roots belong to rye, which has coiled, thread-like roots up to 387 miles (623 km) long.

RYE IS A GRASS GROWN FOR ITS SMALL **FRUITS**, CALLED **CEREAL GRAINS**, WHICH ARE USED TO MAKE BREAD.

 **SUPER SCIENCE**

Scientists believe plants communicate by releasing chemicals through their roots. For example, some chemicals warn surrounding plants of a nearby insect **pest**.

The idea of communication between things that don't have brains is inspiring scientists who design robots to work together in factories. It shows how simple signals can help a group of robots respond to a changing situation.

PSST, PASS IT ON ...

## DO ALL ROOTS GROW IN SOIL?

Some plants have roots that grow aboveground, often wrapping around another plant for support. These roots usually soak up water from the air, so they are more common in misty rainforests. A few, stealthy plants, known as **parasites**, have roots that actually pierce other plants, taking water and nutrients from them.

### KIND OF CLINGY

THIS ORCHID'S ROOTS ARE WRAPPED AROUND A TREE, BUT IT TAKES WATER FROM THE AIR.

### PESKY PARASITE

A MISTLETOE'S ROOTS SUCK WATER AND NUTRIENTS FROM A TREE.

I DON'T EVEN SAY THANK YOU!

## WHY DO SOME PLANTS STRANGLE OTHERS?

Strangler fig trees grow in tall forests where some plants struggle to get enough sunlight. To solve the problem, strangler fig seeds start growing in crevices in the branches of tall trees, where they are dropped by fig-eating birds. As strangler figs get bigger, their roots grow downward, wrapping around their host tree to reach the ground.

I DON'T REMEMBER AGREEING TO THIS ...

# LEAVE IT!

Leaves are busy factories where the work of photosynthesis is done. They take in carbon dioxide from the air through tiny holes called stomata. Water and food are carried through leaves along tubes called veins.

## ARE ALL LEAVES THE SAME?

Leaves have many different shapes and sizes. Scientists divide leaves into basic groups:

### SIMPLE
FOUND ON MANY FLOWERING PLANTS, THESE BROAD, FLAT LEAVES ARE ATTACHED DIRECTLY TO A TWIG OR STEM BY A STALK, CALLED A PETIOLE.

### COMPOUND
ALSO FOUND ON FLOWERING PLANTS, THESE LEAVES HAVE SEVERAL **LEAFLETS** ATTACHED TO THEIR PETIOLE.

### SHEATH
THESE LEAVES WRAP THE STEMS OF GRASSES.

### SCALE
THESE TINY AND POINTY LEAVES, WHICH LOOK A LITTLE LIKE SCALES, ARE FOUND ON CONIFERS, SUCH AS CYPRESSES.

### NEEDLE
FOUND ON CONIFERS SUCH AS FIRS, THESE LEAVES ARE LONG AND THIN.

## WHY DO SOME TREES LOSE THEIR LEAVES IN AUTUMN?

In places with short but cold winters, such as northern parts of the United States, many trees have simple or compound leaves. These soak up sunlight in summer but are too delicate to survive the winter, so they fall to the ground in autumn. Trees that lose their leaves are called **deciduous** trees. In colder places, most trees are conifers with tough, needle-shaped leaves that can survive the long winters.

## WHICH PLANT HAS THE BIGGEST LEAVES?

The biggest leaves, up to 82 feet (25 m) long, grow on the royal raffia palm of tropical regions of Africa. They are compound leaves, made up of 180 leaflets.

### SUPER SCIENCE

Leaves grow from stems in special patterns, often on **alternating** sides or in spirals. These arrangements mean that no leaf is in another's shade.

Solar panels are devices that soak up sunlight to turn it into electricity. The designers of solar panel installations have copied leaf arrangements to make sure their panels catch as much light as possible.

# FIERCE FLOWERS

Flowers are how flowering plants reproduce. They are where male **pollen** meets female **ovules**. From supersized flowers to stinky flowers, they have more to offer than just pretty **petals**.

## ARE FLOWERS MALE OR FEMALE?

Most flowers are both male and female. They have male **stamens** that make pollen. They also have a pistil that contains the female parts. The pistil is made up of a **stigma**, which is sticky to catch pollen; a style, which connects the stigma with the **ovary**; and the ovary, holding ovules. Some plants, such as cucumbers, have flowers that are only male or only female.

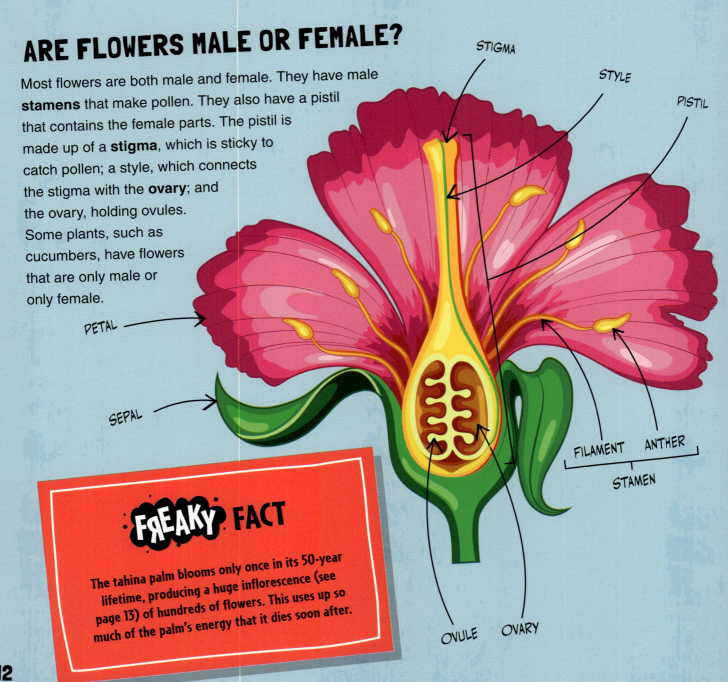

### FREAKY FACT

The tahina palm blooms only once in its 50-year lifetime, producing a huge inflorescence (see page 13) of hundreds of flowers. This uses up so much of the palm's energy that it dies soon after.

# WHICH FLOWER IS THE BIGGEST?

The largest single flower belongs to the corpse flower, named for the fact the bloom smells like rotting meat. The flower reaches 41 inches (105 cm) wide. Some plants produce inflorescences, which are clusters of flowers on a single stem. The largest inflorescence, more than 26 feet (8 m) tall, is made by the titanka plant.

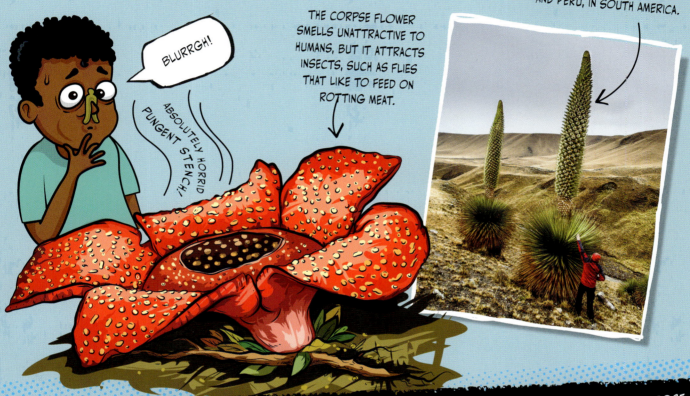

THE TITANKA IS FOUND IN THE ANDES REGIONS OF BOLIVIA AND PERU, IN SOUTH AMERICA.

BLURRGH!

ABSOLUTELY HORRID PUNGENT STENCH!

THE CORPSE FLOWER SMELLS UNATTRACTIVE TO HUMANS, BUT IT ATTRACTS INSECTS, SUCH AS FLIES THAT LIKE TO FEED ON ROTTING MEAT.

# WHICH FLOWER HAS THE MOST PETALS?

The highest number of petals on any wild flower is 12, but garden roses have been **bred** by humans to have more. The flowers of sunflowers and daisies seem to have more petals, but they are actually inflorescences: Their "petals" are separate flowers around a central disk of many more flowers.

GARDEN ROSE

COMMON DAISY

1ST PRIZE

# POWERFUL POLLINATION

Pollination is when pollen is carried from the male parts to the female parts of a flower. Usually pollen is carried to a different flower in the same species. Pollination takes place in strange and surprising ways.

## HOW FAR CAN POLLEN TRAVEL?

Some flowers rely on the wind or on water, such as streams, seas, and rain, to carry their pollen to another flower. When carried by strong winds or oceans, pollen can travel many thousands of miles.

## WHICH ANIMALS ARE POLLINATORS?

Many flowers use animals, called pollinators, to carry their pollen. To attract pollinators, these flowers make nectar, a sugary liquid. When a pollinator feeds on nectar, pollen is caught on their fuzz, fur, or feathers, then rubs off on the next flower they visit. Flowers make sure they attract their particular pollinators by having bright petals, which may also give off an attractive smell. Up to 200,000 different animal species, most of them insects, are pollinators of the 295,000 species of flowering plants.

### HELPFUL HONEYBEE

HONEYBEES USE NECTAR TO MAKE HONEY.

# WHICH FLOWERS GO IT ALONE?

A few flowers pollinate themselves, by having stamens that reach their stigma. These plants often grow in harsh places, such as the Arctic or high mountains, where there are few animals to be pollinators.

*Hi, petal.*

*I would like to be alone.*

*Yum*

### BENEFICIAL BAT
A long-nosed bat drinks from agave blossoms.

### MARVELOUS MOTH
Moths often like pale flowers with a strong smell.

### LOVELY LEMUR
In Madagascar, the black and white ruffed lemur drinks nectar from the traveler's palm plant.

### HANDY HUMMINGBIRD
Hummingbirds have long beaks for sipping nectar.

## FREAKY FACT

The flower of the mirror orchid looks and smells like a female scoliid wasp. Using this trick, it attracts male scoliid wasps to pollinate it.

# WEIRD FRUIT

After pollination, a flower's ovules turn into seeds, and its ovary becomes a fruit. The fruit may be fleshy, as in a plum, or hard, as in a nut. Some fruits, such as raspberries, are made of several ovaries joined together.

## ARE ALL FRUITS EDIBLE?

Many fruits are tiny, dry, or poisonous to humans. Yet lots of fruits – from apples to bananas – are healthy to eat and taste sweetly delicious. Some edible fruits are **savory**-tasting: cucumbers, tomatoes, and wheat grains are also fruits. For a plant, producing edible fruits is a way to spread its seeds far and wide, so that baby plants do not grow in their parent's shadow. After munching on a fruit, an animal spits or poops out the seeds, which can then start to grow.

*IN ONE END ...*

*PLOP*

*... AND OUT THE OTHER ... YIPPEE!*

### FREAKY FACT

Rather than waiting to be eaten, the fruit of the sandbox tree explodes when it is ripe. The seeds are thrown up to 148 feet (45 m) from the tree.

**BOOM!**

# WHICH FRUIT SMELLS LIKE POOP ... OR CUSTARD?

In Southeast Asia, the durian fruit is known for its strong smell, which attracts animals including tigers and orangutans from nearly a mile away. While some people describe the smell as like custard or caramel, others describe it as poop, vomit, or rotten onions. These different responses are due to the fruit's complex mix of chemicals.

THE DURIAN'S THORNY COATING DISCOURAGES SMALL ANIMALS, BUT LARGE ANIMALS CAN BREAK OPEN THE FRUIT, THEN CARRY ITS SEEDS FAR AWAY.

MMM, CUSTARD.

EWW, POOP.

# WHICH FRUIT HAS THE MOST SEEDS?

The pomegranate fruit has the most seeds, up to 1,400. It is produced from a single ovary that contains many ovules. At the other end of the scale, a few plants can produce fruits without being pollinated, making seedless fruits that cannot grow into new plants. Seedless fruits are easy to eat, so humans sometimes grow more of these plants by cutting **sprigs** and planting them. That is why we have seedless mandarins!

COUNT MY SEEDS! GO ON!

# STRANGE SEEDS

Inside a tough coating, a seed holds an unformed baby plant and a little food. A seed will not start to sprout until it is in a suitable spot. Plants have weird ways of helping their seeds find that spot.

## WHAT STRANGE METHODS DO PLANTS USE TO SPREAD SPEEDS?

Edible fruits are not the only method of spreading seeds over a wide area:

**TUMBLING**

TUMBLEWEED PLANTS SEPARATE FROM THEIR ROOTS SO THEY CAN BE BLOWN ALONG, SPREADING SEEDS AS THEY GO.

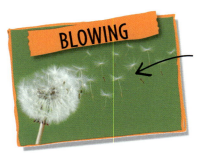

**BLOWING**

AFTER POLLINATION, DANDELION FLOWERS TURN INTO **SEEDHEADS** WITH MANY TINY FRUITS, EACH ATTACHED TO A SUPERLIGHT UMBRELLA TO LIFT IT ON THE WIND.

**FLOATING**

PLANTS THAT LIVE BY RIVERS OR OCEANS OFTEN PRODUCE FLOATING FRUITS OR SEEDS.

**ANTS!**

SOME PLANTS MAKE SEEDS WITH FLESHY LUMPS ATTACHED TO THEM. ANTS COLLECT THE SEEDS, EAT THE LUMPS, THEN LEAVE THE SEEDS TO GROW.

# WHY ARE FORGETFUL SQUIRRELS USEFUL?

Squirrels like to eat nuts, which are hard fruits. When acorns and hazelnuts ripen in autumn, squirrels bury some to eat during winter. The problem for squirrels is that they forget where they buried all their nuts! But the lost acorns and hazelnuts may grow into oak and hazel trees.

*NOW WHERE DID I LEAVE IT ...?*

# WHICH SEED TOOK LONGEST TO START GROWING?

Seeds do not start to grow, or germinate, until the levels of warmth and water are just right. Water or heat cracks the seed's coating after a few days, weeks, or even years. The seeds that took the longest to germinate belonged to date palms. They were left in desert caves in what is now Israel, around 2,000 years ago. After being found by scientists, the seeds were soaked and planted, then grew into trees.

## SUPER SCIENCE

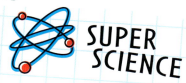

A bur is a seed or dry fruit that is covered in hooks. The hooks catch on animal fur, so the seed can hitch a ride away from its parent plant. In 1941, Swiss inventor George de Mestral was walking in the woods when he noticed how burs clung to his clothes and his dog's fur. They inspired him to invent Velcro®, a system for fastening clothes and shoes using two strips, one with tiny hooks and the other with loops.

*I'M WORTH WAITING FOR.*

A DATE PALM GROWS CLUSTERS OF SWEET FRUIT.

# KILLER PLANTS

Some plants are not content with quietly turning sunlight into food. They need something a little bit more ... wiggly ... to keep them going. These plants use dirty tricks to meet their need for meat!

## WHY DO THEY KILL?

Meat-eating plants grow in soil that is thin or swampy, so it does not contain enough nutrients to keep them healthy. They get extra nutrients from the bodies of unlucky little animals!

YIKES!

## WHAT TRICKS AND TRAPS DO THEY USE?

First of all, a meat-eating plant needs to attract insects and other little creatures. It manages this with its sweet nectar, yummy smell, or bright color. Then the plant may use one of these clever – and very cruel – traps:

### THE STICKY END
PREY IS CAUGHT ON STICKY LEAVES.

### DEATH SLIDE
PREY FALLS INTO A SLIPPERY BOWL-LIKE TRAP MADE FROM A ROLLED-UP LEAF.

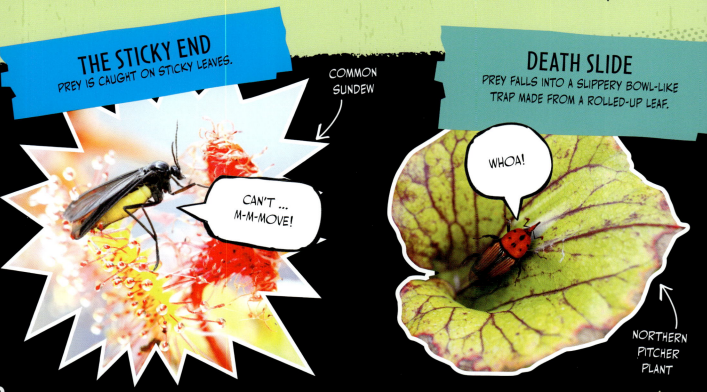

COMMON SUNDEW

CAN'T ... M-M-MOVE!

WHOA!

NORTHERN PITCHER PLANT

# WHAT IS THE BIGGEST ANIMAL A PLANT CAN EAT?

The bigger the plant, the bigger the prey! The giant pitcher plant has a slippery bowl-shaped trap up to 16 inches (40 cm) high and 8 inches (20 cm) wide. Ants and other insects are its usual food, but birds, frogs, lizards, and rats can all drown in the rainwater and digestive liquids that fill its deadly trap.

IF HIKING THROUGH THE RAINFOREST OF BORNEO IN SOUTHEAST ASIA, WATCH OUT FOR THE GIANT PITCHER PLANT.

## SUPER SCIENCE

Scientists were so impressed by the slipperiness of pitcher plants that they decided to copy them. Teams are working on new super-slippery coatings, called SLIPS (short for slippery liquid-infused porous surfaces), for boats, machines, and medical instruments. The coatings will stop sea creatures, dirt, ice, or oil from getting stuck on them.

### THE CRUSHER
PREY MAKES THE MISTAKE OF TICKLING THE HAIRS ON HINGED LEAVES, WHICH SNAP CLOSED.

### NO WAY OUT
PREY CRAWLS INSIDE A COILED LEAF, THEN CANNOT FIND THE EXIT.

"THAT DIDN'T GO WELL!"

VENUS FLYTRAP

EXHAUSTED BY SEARCHING FOR THE WAY OUT, THE INSECT WILL EVENTUALLY TUMBLE INTO THIS COBRA LILY'S "STOMACH." IT WILL BE BROKEN DOWN BY SPECIAL DIGESTIVE LIQUIDS, THEN SOAKED UP.

"I'M IN HERE!"

# DON'T EAT ME!

Many plants put up with being nibbled by plant-eaters, but others have developed defenses to stop themselves from being lunch. These defenses range from tough bark on tree trunks to stings, prickles, and poisons.

THE STINGING BRUSH GROWS IN AUSTRALIAN RAINFORESTS. DON'T BE TEMPTED TO TOUCH IT!

## WHICH PLANT HAS THE MOST POWERFUL STING?

The stinging brush, or stinging tree, is covered by stinging hairs. If they are touched, the hollow, sharp hairs break off and enter the skin. They inject a chemical that can cause pain for days. There are accounts of the pain from the sting coming back months or even years later.

## WHICH CACTUS IS NO TEDDY BEAR?

The teddy bear cactus has long, sharp **spines**. If they get stuck in the skin of an animal, they are extremely difficult and painful to remove, because they have tiny hooks. From a distance, the spines make the cactus look furry, which earned the plant its name.

TEDDY BEAR CACTUS

# WHICH PLANT IS THE DEADLIEST?

Many plants have poisonous fruits, seeds, or other parts. The competition for the deadliest plant is fierce:

**ROSARY PEA** — THESE SEEDS ARE SOMETIMES USED AS BEADS, BUT ARE DEADLY IF EATEN.

**DEADLY NIGHTSHADE** — BOTH LEAVES AND BERRIES ARE POISONOUS.

**WATER HEMLOCK** — ALL PARTS ARE POISONOUS, BUT THE ROOTS ARE DEADLIEST.

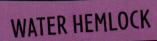

**TOBACCO** — THE DRIED LEAVES ARE USED IN CIGARETTES, WHICH CAN CAUSE CANCER AND HEART AND LUNG DISEASES.

## FREAKY FACT

The plant with the longest thorns, over 8 inches (20 cm) long, is the North American honey locust. Thorns are branches or stems that, over millions of years, have evolved to be sharp.

# FUNKY FEEDERS

We should all eat plenty of plant parts in the form of cereal grains, fruits, and **vegetables**. These give us energy, protein for growing, vitamins and minerals for health, and **fiber** to help keep our digestive systems healthy.

## WHICH PLANT DO HUMANS EAT MOST?

The small, dry fruit of the rice plant is the food most eaten by humans. Across much of the world, rice is a staple food, which is a food eaten often and in large quantities. Close behind rice are two other cereal grains: maize and wheat.

I'M FEEDING THE WORLD!

## WHICH PART OF A PLANT IS A VEGETABLE?

The foods we call vegetables come from many different plant parts:

### ROOTS
CARROTS ARE SWOLLEN ROOTS, WHERE THE PLANT STORES FOOD TO SURVIVE WINTER.

### STEMS
POTATOES ARE SWOLLEN UNDERGROUND STEMS, CALLED TUBERS, WHICH LAST THROUGH WINTER WHEN THE ABOVEGROUND PLANT DIES. THEY CAN GROW INTO A NEW PLANT IN SPRING.

### BULBS
ONIONS ARE SWOLLEN UNDERGROUND STEMS AND LEAVES, CALLED BULBS.

# HOW MANY SEEDS IN A BAR OF CHOCOLATE?

Around 50 seeds, called cocoa beans, go into making one snack-sized bar of chocolate, along with milk, sugar, and oil. Around 30 to 50 seeds form in each pod on a cocoa (or cacao) tree. The tree grows naturally only in hot parts of the Americas, but is today also grown in Africa and Asia.

*ONE GIANT LEAP FOR SPUD-KIND.*

*I LOVE SEEDS ...*

## SUPER SCIENCE

In 1995, astronauts first experimented with growing potatoes in space, aboard the Space Shuttle *Columbia*. Scientists are now figuring out how plants could be grown on Mars, where the air contains carbon dioxide but very little oxygen. Since plants make oxygen, plants might be a way to create an oxygen supply for future inhabitants of the distant planet.

**LEAVES** — LETTUCES ARE FLOPPY, CRISPY, OR CURLY LEAVES.

**FRUITS** — TOMATOES ARE FRUITS, EVEN THOUGH THEY TASTE SAVORY.

**SEEDS** — PEAS ARE SEEDS THAT GROW IN A FRUIT CALLED A POD.

# ODDLY USEFUL

Trees give wood for homes, furniture, and paper. Roses and lavender scent soaps and perfume, while acacia makes glue. You are surrounded by plants, from your clothes to your medicine cabinet.

*I HAVE HIDDEN POWERS ...*

## WHICH MEDICINES ARE MADE FROM PLANTS?

The earliest medicines were made when people noticed that some plants helped treat fevers or wounds. Many modern medicines are still made with chemicals that come from plants, including the opium poppy, which can ease pain, and the Madagascar periwinkle, which helps treat cancer.

LIKE MOST MEDICINAL PLANTS, THE OPIUM POPPY IS BOTH USEFUL AND EXTREMELY DANGEROUS.

## CAN PLANTS POWER CARS?

Most cars are powered by burning a **fuel** called oil in their engine. Since burning oil also pollutes the air, people are looking for fuels that are cleaner. One solution may be sugarcane, which can be used to make a liquid fuel that often powers cars in Brazil.

*AREN'T YOU HUNGRY?*

# WHICH PLANTS DO WE WEAR?

Plant fibers, or threads, can be woven, knitted, or braided into fabric:

THE FLUFFY SEEDHEADS OF THE COTTON PLANT ARE SPUN INTO COTTON.

LINEN IS MADE OF STEM FIBERS FROM THE FLAX PLANT.

**COTTON**

**FLAX**

**BAMBOO**

**PANAMA HAT PLANT**

THE LEAVES OF THE PANAMA HAT PLANT ARE USED TO WEAVE … HATS.

BAMBOO IS A STIFF-STEMMED GRASS USED TO MAKE CLOTH.

## FREAKY FACT

Bamboo is the fastest-growing plant, growing up to 35 inches (91 cm) per day. In addition to clothing, bamboo stems are used for furniture, toothbrushes, and utensils.

BAMBOO

# ASTONISHING ACTIVITY: COLORFUL LEAVES

Try this experiment using chromatography (which means "color writing" in Greek). It is a method of separating the parts of mixtures. You will find out if leaves contain only green chlorophyll or a colorful mixture.

### YOU WILL NEED::

10 GREEN LEAVES

A GLASS

RUBBING ALCOHOL (AND AN ADULT'S HELP TO USE IT)

A CLOTHESPIN

A WOODEN SPOON

A BOWL OF HOT TAP WATER (AND AN ADULT'S HELP)

A LONG STRIP OF PAPER TOWEL OR COFFEE FILTER PAPER

1. Rip the leaves into small pieces, then place them in your glass.

2. Ask an adult to help you add enough rubbing alcohol to just cover the leaves. The rubbing alcohol will start to break down the leaves.

**3** Crush the leaves into the rubbing alcohol using the blunt end of a wooden spoon.

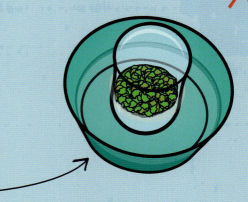

**4** Without getting water inside the glass, place the glass in a bowl of hot tap water to speed things along. Put the bowl and glass in a dark place, such as a cupboard, for 30 minutes or until the rubbing alcohol has turned dark green.

**5** Gently stir your green mixture, then place the strip of paper towel in the glass, with just the tip of one end in the mixture. Secure it with a clothespin if needed.

**6** Watch for around 30 minutes as the paper soaks up the liquid. What is happening to the color of the strip? When one of the colors reaches the top of the strip, remove the strip, and let it dry.

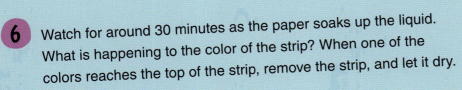

## COLORFUL CONCLUSION

The chemicals in the leaves, called **pigments**, **dissolve** in the rubbing alcohol, so specks of pigments are floating in the liquid. As the paper soaks up the liquid, the pigments are carried with it. Some travel further up the paper because their specks are smaller and lighter. Once the pigments are separated, you can see green, yellow, and orange. This experiment tells us about what happens to the leaves of deciduous trees in autumn. As the leaves stop photosynthesizing, their chlorophyll breaks down, revealing the colors that are usually hidden by the overpowering green.

# GLOSSARY

**absorb** to soak up

**alternating** occurring by turns

**bred** grown to have particular characteristics by choosing which plants should reproduce with each other

**carbon dioxide** an invisible gas found in the air that plants take in and humans expel

**cereal grain** an edible, dry fruit produced by grasses such as rice, wheat, oats, and maize

**chlorophyll** a green pigment found in plants that absorbs sunlight for photosynthesis

**deciduous** shedding leaves every year

**dissolve** to mix into a liquid

**embryo** a developing baby

**evolve** to change slowly over millions of years

**fiber** parts of plants that the human body cannot digest, or break down

**flower** the part of a seed-making plant that contains the reproductive parts

**fruit** the part of a plant that contains seeds and may be edible or inedible

**fuel** a material that can be burned to produce heat

**habitat** the natural home of a plant or animal

**leaf** a green part of a plant, where photosynthesis usually takes place, that is joined at one end to a stem or stalk

**leaflet** a small leaf-like structure forming part of a compound leaf

**nutrient** a substance taken in by a living thing that is needed for growth and life

**ovary** in plants, a female reproductive part that will develop into a fruit

**ovule** the part of an ovary that will develop into a seed

**oxygen** an invisible gas that is made by plants and breathed in by humans

**parasite** a living thing that lives on or in another living thing and takes food from it

**pest** an insect or other animal that attacks crops

**petal** a special, usually colorful, plant part that surrounds the reproductive parts of a flower

**photosynthesis** the process by which plants produce food from sunlight, carbon dioxide, and water

**pigment** a material that produces color

**pollen** a powder, made by the male parts of a flower, that causes the female parts of the same species to make seeds

**reproduce** to make new young plants

**root** the part of a plant that anchors it in position and takes in water and nutrients

**savory** tasting salty or spicy but not sweet

**seed** a small object made by a plant that can grow into a new plant

**seedhead** the seed-containing part of some plants that develops after flowering or fruiting

**species** a group of living things that look similar to each other and can reproduce together

**spine** a sharp-pointed growth

**sprig** a small stem taken from a plant

**stamen** a male, pollen-making part of a flower

**stem** the main body of a plant

**stigma** a female part of a flower, where pollen is received

**vascular** containing special structures for carrying water and food through the plant

**vegetable** any edible plant part with a savory taste

**vein** a structure that carries water and food through a leaf

# FURTHER READING

## BOOKS

*The Kew Gardens Children's Cookbook: Plant, Cook, Eat,*
Caroline Craig (Wayland, 2016)

*Plants* (Outdoor Science),
Sonya Newland (Wayland, 2018)

*Plants* (Science in Infographics),
Jon Richards and Ed Simkins (Wayland, 2017)

*Plants* (Science Skills Sorted),
Angela Royston (Franklin Watts, 2019)

*Studying Plants* (Citizen Scientist),
Izzi Howell (Wayland, 2020)

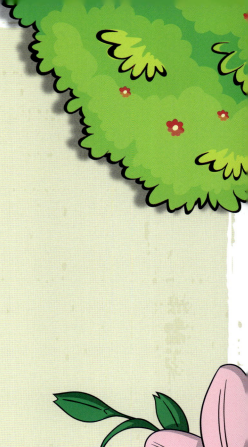

## WEBSITES

Find out more about plants on these websites:

**kids.britannica.com/kids/article/plant/353639**

**www.bbc.co.uk/bitesize/topics/zy66fg8**

**www.gardenersworld.com/how-to/grow-plants/10-gardening-projects-for-kids/**

**www.worldwildlife.org/places/amazon**

# INDEX

bamboo 27
bees 14
burs 19

cacti 4, 22
carbon dioxide 4, 10, 25
cereal grains 8, 24
chlorophyll 4, 28, 29
chocolate 25
communication 8
cones 7
conifers 7, 10, 11
corpse flower 13
cotton 27

daisies 13
dandelions 18
deadly nightshade 23
deciduous trees 11, 29

fabrics 27
ferns 4, 6, 7
flowering plants 5, 7, 10, 12–13, 14–15, 16–17, 18
fruit 8, 16–17, 18, 19, 23, 24, 25
fuel 26

hummingbirds 15

inflorescences 12, 13

leaves 6, 7, 10–11, 20, 21, 23, 24, 25, 27, 28–29

maize 24
meat-eating plants 20–21
medicines 26
mosses 7

nectar 14, 15, 20
nitrogen 8
nutrients 8, 9, 20
nuts 16, 19

orchids 9, 15
oxygen 4, 5, 25

parasites 9
photosynthesis 4, 5, 10, 29
poisonous plants 16, 23
pollination 14–15, 16, 18
potatoes 24, 25

rice 24
roots 6, 7, 8–9, 18, 23, 24

seeds 7, 9, 16, 17, 18–19, 23, 25
smells 13, 14, 15, 17, 20
spines 22
spores 7
squirrels 19
stinging plants 22
strangler fig 9
sunlight 4, 5, 6, 9, 11

tobacco 23
trees 4, 5, 6, 9, 11, 16, 19, 22, 25, 26, 29

vascular plants 6, 7
vegetables 24–25

water 4, 6, 7, 8, 9, 10, 14, 19, 21
wheat 16, 24
wood 5, 26